GEARED FOR GROWTH BIBLE STUDIES

FAITH THAT WORKS

A STUDY IN JAMES

BIBLE STUDIES TO IMPACT THE LIVES OF ORDINARY PEOPLE

Christian Focus Publications

The Word Worldwide

Written by Marie Dinnen

CONTENTS

QUESTIONS AND NOTES

ANSWER GUIDE

PREFACE

GEARED FOR GROWTH

Where there's LIFE there's GROWTH:
Where there's GROWTH there's LIFE.'

WHY GROW a study group?

Because as we study the Bible and share together we can

- learn to combat loneliness, depression, staleness, frustration, and other problems
- get to understand and love each other
- become responsive to the Holy Spirit's dealing and obedient to God's Word

and that's GROWTH.

How do you GROW a study group?

- Just start by asking a friend to join you and then aim at expanding your group.
- Study the set portions daily (they are brief and easy: no catches).
- Meet once a week to discuss what you find.
- Befriend others, both Christians and non Christians, and work away together

see how it GROWS!

WHEN you GROW ...

This will happen at school, at home, at work, at play, in your youth group, your student fellowship, women's meetings, mid-week meetings, churches and communities,

you'll be REACHING THROUGH TEACHING

INTRODUCTORY STUDY

Which James wrote the letter?
Three different men, all named James, are mentioned in Luke 6:14-16; Matthew 10:2-3 and Matthew 4:21. Since the first two have no other mention in Scripture and the third was martyred some years before the epistle is estimated to have been written, historians rule out the possibility of them being responsible for the writing.

A fourth James is mentioned, however, and tradition holds that he is the author of the book. Look up the references given and discuss what you find out about him.

Who was he? See Matthew 13:55; Mark 6:3; Galatians 1:19.
Who appeared to him? (Despite Acts 10:41) I Corinthians 15:7.
Did he have leadership ability? Acts 12:17; Galatians 1:19.
What title does Paul give him? Galatians 2:9.
Does he speak with knowledge and authority? Acts 15:13-21.

What does he say?
The core of James' message is stated in James 1:4 - 'So let it (patience) grow, and don't try to squirm out of your problems. For when your patience is finally in full bloom, then you will be ready for anything, strong in character, full and complete' (LB).

The key word is MATURE. James speaks out against the spiritually immature characteristics which marred the testimony of some of these early Jewish Christians.

'James warns against corrupt partiality;
Exhorts to practise Christian charity;
Faith without works is dead he clearly shows;
The tree is judged by the kind of fruit it grows.'

To whom does he say it?
James has been called the New Testament Amos. Where Amos warned the Israelites against imbibing the sloth, godlessness and materialism of surrounding nations, James writing from Jerusalem, warns Christian Jews throughout Asia not to be discouraged when tests and trials come upon them (vv. 2-3). He does not write as an evangelist so much as a Christian encouraging his brethren.

Are you impatient?

Amos   OT   867

James 1:2 and 5:7 say: 'Consider it pure joy, my brothers whenever you face trials of many kinds ... Be patient, then, brothers, until the Lord's coming. See how the farmer waits for the land to yield its valuable crop and how patient he is for the autumn and spring rains.'

The Bible stresses patience as a quality of Christian character. You could find much encouragement by looking up and reading all the Bible references associated with patience (forbearance and long-suffering mean the same). Here are a few to whet your appetite:–

Romans 2:7; 12:12	I Corinthians 13:4	Colossians 3:12
I Thessalonians 5:14	I Timothy 6:11	Hebrews 6:12; 10:36
Hebrews 12:1.		

If you are lacking in patience why not pray this right now?

'Lord Jesus, you know patience isn't my strong point. I often get angry and irritated with others and this mars my testimony. You were never impatient with people. No matter how tired you were, you gave yourself to them. Teach me as I study this book to accept all the trying circumstances of life and make them stepping stones into all the grace and patience that should be manifest in my life. For your Name's sake. Amen .'

Note that the Greek *word* used for patience is *hupomone*. It literally means 'an abiding under' from hupo (under) and *meno* (to abide). In modern language we could say 'sticking with it'.

STUDY 1

HOW TO GROW

Tues 13th Jan

QUESTIONS

DAY 1 *P.276 NT,*
James 1:1-4; Matthew 5:48.
a) What kind of person is a Christian to be?

b) I Corinthians 3:1-7. List some of the products of a
spiritually immature life. *(p 199 NT)*

DAY 2 *James 1:1-4; 2 Peter 3:18. (P 289 NT).*
a) What is essential to spiritual growth or maturity (even
before the testings)?

b) *P 113 NT*
John 1:11-14. What do these verses emphasise about
becoming part of God's family?

DAY 3 *R113 TP. 276   p 231 N.T.*
James 1:2,19; Ephesians 3:14-15; 4:25.
a) How does James identify himself with other Christians?

Albar

b) From the 'Ephesian' references, what are some of the
privileges and responsibilities of being in God's Family?

DAY 4 *James 1:1.*
a) What title did James give himself?

b) I Corinthians 6:19-20; I Peter 1:18-19. Why are Christians
to see themselves as servants or slaves of the Lord Jesus?

QUESTIONS (contd.)

DAY 5 *James 1:1; 4:7, 10.*
a) As a servant what did James ask other Christians to do?

b) Ephesians 4:2; Philippians 2:3-4. How are our relationships with others affected when we are truly humble?

DAY 6 *James 1:2-4,12; Hebrews 12:5-7; I Peter 1:7.*
a) Why does God allow His children to be tried?

b) Can you say you rejoice when trouble hits you?

DAY 7 *James 1:12; Matthew 5:10-12.*
a) What encouragement is there to persevere under trials?

b) What does God expect of His children even in trials (Jas. 1:12b)?

NOTES

1. *Make sure you are alive*
Only living things grow. By nature we are dead in 'transgressions and sins' (Eph. 2:1) but we can come alive in Christ (1 Cor. 15:22). If you have reached first base (John 1:12) then 2 Peter 3:18 is for you.

2. *Recognise your relations*
Notice that James takes for granted that his readers are part of God's family ('brothers' in v. 2). Just as in a human family we talk, work, share together, so we are to recognise our privileges of being in Christ and fulfil our obligations by loving, caring for and encouraging each other. (See Rom. 12:10; Heb. 13:1; 2 Pet. 1:7).

3. *Learn to be humble*
James calls himself a servant (v. 1). He could have boasted that he was the brother of Jesus or the Bishop of Jerusalem. Submission is another term for humility and we are told to be submissive to God (Jas. 4:7, 10) and to one another (Phil. 2:3-8). The bondslave refused his freedom out of love for his master and gave up all rights to himself, willingly pledging servitude for the rest of his life. Do you love Jesus enough to become his bondslave? Such 'slavery' brings rich rewards in fellowship, joy and love.

4. *Look positively at trials and testing*
See them as stepping stones to maturity, to strengthen faith. Don't get 'thrown for a loop' when trials come 'out of the blue' (v. 2). We never know what is round the corner. Think of Job, Paul and all those mentioned in Hebrews 11. Trials of all kinds came to them: torture, beatings, loss of loved ones, loss of home, belongings, friends; loneliness, hardship and perplexity; but nothing daunted their faith. They learned to recognise that God was using these circumstances to prove He loved them (Heb. 12:6) and planned only blessing for them (Rom. 8:28). Never give up under trial for the results are always sure (v. 4). Faith brings its rewards. Look at verse 12. It's for YOU,

'Don't be submerged in the PROCESS, look towards the finished PRODUCT.'

STUDY 2

HOW TO BE REALLY WISE

27th Jan

QUESTIONS

DAY 1 *James 1:5; 3:13-18.*
a) What two kinds of wisdom are there?

b) List the end products of each kind. Which one is preferable?

DAY 2 *James 1:5.*
a) What encouragement is there to seek true wisdom?

b) Philippians 4:19. What was Paul confident God would do?

DAY 3 *James 1:6-8; 4:8.*
a) What will hinder God from answering our prayers?

clean

b) Mark 12:30; Hebrews 11:6. What are we encouraged to do in these verses?

DAY 4 *James 1:9-11; Matthew 6:19-20; 1 Timothy 6:17-19.* p 255
a) What two types of Christian are referred to? What advice is given to each type?

b) How does the parable in Luke 12:13-21 tragically illustrate James 1:11?

9

QUESTIONS (contd.)

DAY 5 *James 1:13-15; Matthew 4:3; 1 Thessalonians 3:5.*
a) Who tempts us to do evil?

b) How does temptation master us?

DAY 6 *James 1:13-15; 1 Corinthians 10:13; Hebrews 4:15-16; James 4:7.*
a) Why would people blame God for tempting them to evil? What does James clearly say about this?

b) How are we to overcome temptation?

DAY 7 *James 1:16-18; Colossians 2:2-4; 3:16.*
a) What does James teach us about God?

b) How can we avoid being deceived?

NOTES

Did James write: 'If you feel your lack of wisdom, keep going to college. Go for more degrees'? No. He rather underlines 1 Corinthians 13:8: 'knowledge ... will pass away' and stresses the all-importance of spiritual wisdom which produces Christian character.

Education is valuable and we should aspire after knowledge. But how futile if we don't have the wisdom to make that knowledge work! It is possible to be knowledgeable about computers, medical science, art skills, aerodynamics, etc. and yet to be abysmally ignorant of the truth which can make us 'wise for salvation' (2 Tim. 3:15).

Temptation is the devil's way of stumbling a Christian. He tempted Eve with the lure of a rival source of knowledge and status equal to God if she disobeyed God (Gen. 3:2-6). Eve was dazzled by this magnificent serpent (not yet cursed to crawl – Gen. 3:14) and by the delicious 'fruit of independence' (Gen. 3:6) placed before her.

Romans 6:16 indicates that our human desires and appetites can respond either to good or evil domination. It is only as we yield to Satan or God that our lives produce the fruit of that union. God has made full provision for His children, through Christ, that they may overcome the tempter and, submitting to God, produce the good fruits of righteousness in our lives. See the contrast between Galatians 5:19-21 and 5:22-26.

Why don't you read a chapter of Proverbs each day for a month or two and see what God will teach you about wisdom? Read Proverbs 1:2-5; 2:1-6; 3:1-2 in various translations.

Steps to Heavenly Wisdom
1. *Realise your need.* When you are prepared to honestly admit you can't run your life the wisest thing to do is to turn to God who alone can meet your need (Phil. 4:19).

2. *Ask God for Wisdom.* He is the source and able to do much more than we could ever ask (Eph. 3:20). If we ask, we will receive (1 John 3:22).

3. *Believe Him for it.* God never breaks His Word (Matt. 24:35). What He promises He will do (Titus 1:2). But His promises only become effective when we trust Him and persevere (Heb. 6:12). James 1:5 says He gives without reserve and without reproach.

Psalm 107 tells of His wisdom and steadfast love to the Israelites. Can you say that verse 43 applies to you? The last verse applies to all those who come in humility and penitence, acknowledging their need: 'Whoever is wise, let him heed these things and consider the great love of the LORD.'

STUDY 3
THE WORD OF GOD

QUESTIONS

DAY 1 *James 1:18; John 3:3; 1 Corinthians 15:20-23.*
a) Refer to the questions for Day 2 in Study 1. What does James emphasise about being born again?

b) What are the 'firstfruits' a sign of?

DAY 2 *James 1:19-20; Colossians 3:8; Ephesians 4:26,31.*
a) Do you find James 1:19 difficult to put into practice?

b) What is wrong with 'man's anger'?

DAY 3 *James 1:18-21; 1 Peter 2:1-2.*
a) What complementary teaching is found in these two passages?

b) John 15:4-8. If God's Word really takes root in us, what happens?

DAY 4 *James 1:22; Luke 6:46-49.*
a) According to James, what is happening when we are merely 'listening' to God's Word?

b) How did Jesus warn against merely 'listening' to His teaching?

QUESTIONS (contd.)

DAY 5 *James 1:23-24; Deuteronomy 4:8-9; 2 Peter 1:8-9.*
a) To what is God's Word likened in James?

b) How is the casual hearer described?

DAY 6 *James 1:25.*
a) What encouragement is there for 'doers' of God's Word? What distinguishes them from mere 'listeners'?

b) Psalm 1:1-6. What results here from obeying God's Word?

DAY 7 *James 1:26-27; Matthew 12:33-35.*
a) How do our tongues give us away?

b) What two things are to characterise the Christian?

NOTES

James shows us that it is quite impossible to live in a way that pleases the Lord unless we apply ourselves daily to the Word of God and make its teaching operative in our daily lives. The Word is the instrument whereby the Holy Spirit brings us to life in Christ (Jas. 1:18). Look up 1 Peter 1:23 and Romans 10:17 and see how Peter and Paul major on its importance too. James describes the Word in three ways:

THE WORD OF TRUTH (Jas. 1:18). God's word is unique. The *whole* Bible is the truth and the *whole* truth of God (see Ps. 119:43, 160). God's Word *alone* is *truth* (John 17:17).

THE PLANTED (ENGRAFTED) WORD (Jas. 1:21). God's Word is *living* and therefore life-giving when planted in our hearts (1 Pet. 1:23).

THE PERFECT LAW (Jas. 1:25). Coming from a *perfect* source, this perfect Word of Truth makes the receiver perfect or mature (2 Tim. 3:15-17). As we make it the law or rule of our life (Deut. 10:12-13 and Ps. 19:7-8) it becomes a liberating force, setting us free to serve the Living God (see 1 Thess. 1:8-9).

HEAR AND DO

Here is some practical advice on how to respond to God's Word. From verses 21-26 we see we are to *receive, obey, study* and *adjust our lives* by the Word of God. If we look in a mirror and see that our faces are dirty, we automatically head for soap and water. Likewise if we see our sinful selves reflected in the mirror of God's Word we should act accordingly. (See 2 Cor. 7:1; Eph. 4:22-32; Heb. 12:1; 1 Pet. 2:1-3.)

DECEIVED

If we pick out certain words and expressions from verses 26-27 they fall into two categories. Where do we stand?

Marks of True Religion	*Marks of False Religion*
Controlled Tongue (Ps. 141:3)	Seemingly religious (Matt. 6:1-7)
Compassionate Heart (Eph. 4:32)	Self deceived (2 Cor. 4:3-4)
Consecrated Life (2 Tim. 2:21)	Vain (2 Tim. 3:1-5)

What does God want of us? You will find His desire in Deuteronomy 5:29 and again in Micah 6:8.

STUDY 4
FAITH IN ACTION

QUESTIONS

DAY 1 *James 2:1-4.*
a) What sin is being condemned here and how did it manifest itself?

b) What other types of discrimination should we be aware of and avoid today?

DAY 2 *James 2:5-7.*
a) What arguments are given in favour of according better treatment to the poor?

b) What particular form of persecution is highlighted in verse 7 and also in Revelation 13:5-6?

DAY 3 *James 2:8-13.*
a) What law is the Christian to always live by?

b) How does James dismiss the artificial distinction we are sometimes tempted to make between serious sins such as murder, and seemingly not so serious ones such as showing favouritism?

DAY 4 *James 2:14-19.*
a) Why are Christians not to be so heavenly minded as to be of no earthly use?

QUESTIONS (contd.)

b) On what grounds does God accept us? Do we have to do anything good to be saved (Luke 18:13-14; Titus 2:5)?

DAY 5 *James 2:14,20-24; Genesis 22:9-12; Hebrews 11:17-19.*
a) What is the PROOF of our faith?

b) How did Abraham PROVE he had faith?

DAY 6 *James 2:14,25-26; Joshua 2:6-11; 6:25.*
a) Why did Rahab hide the spies?

b) How was her faith rewarded?

DAY 7 *Luke 19:8; Acts 16:14-15; 16:30-34.*
a) How did these three people demonstrate their faith?

b) How does James say we are to demonstrate our faith?

NOTES

We should remember in studying this chapter that James is addressing Christians. He points out not what they have to DO to become Christians, but how to ACT because they *are* Christians.

It is important that we look again at the Scriptures which establish the basis of our salvation (e.g. Is. 45:22; John 10:9; Acts 4:12; etc.). We should be firmly convinced that:

Salvation is to be found in Christ alone (John 14:6),
Salvation is a gift of God (Rom. 6:23; Eph. 2:8),
Salvation cannot be earned (Titus 3:5; Eph. 2:8).

Practical James states that there is no use *saying* you believe unless you act accordingly. In Mark 10:17-22 we read about the rich young ruler. He *knew* a lot about Jesus. He *believed* he ought to keep God's commandments. But when he was put to the test he wasn't willing to *trust* himself and all he had to Christ.

On the other hand, the woman in Mark 5:25-29 *knew* about Jesus, *believed* He could heal her and *trusted* Him to do so.

James tells us that since we belong to Christ our lives should add up:

- We should show unbiased Christian love to others, not giving deference to those who have material wealth and ignoring those who are not so well-off (Jas. 2:1-7).
- We should love others as we love ourselves (Jas. 2:8).
- We should demonstrate our love by helping to alleviate the needs of others (Jas. 2:14-18).
- We should take note of those whose lives set forth faith in action and beware lest our professed faith is just sham (Jas. 2:21-26).

Look up Psalm 37:3, 27. Here God promises His blessing on those who: 'Trust in the Lord and do good' and 'Turn from evil and do good'.

Spurgeon once said: 'Trust in God sets us about doing good. We trust Him for salvation and then we do good. We don't just sit still because we trust, we rouse ourselves and *expect* God to work in and through us. It's not for us to worry and do evil, but to trust and do good. We neither trust without doing nor do without trusting.'

Is your FAITH in ACTION?

STUDY 5
WISE TEACHERS AND WISE TONGUES

QUESTIONS

DAY 1 *James 3:1.*
a) What warning is given specifically to teachers here?

b) Ephesians 4:11. What assurance should a teacher of the Word have?

DAY 2 *James 3:2; Romans 3:10-14; Mark 7:21-23.*
a) How do the things we say give us away?

b) What does James 3:2 say about the person who can control his tongue?

DAY 3 *James 3:3-5; Read verse 4 in several translations.*
a) What is significant about the size and function of a bit, rudder and tongue?

b) How is a big ship in a fierce storm controlled?

DAY 4 *James 3:5-8; Matthew 5:22; 12:34-37.*
a) What does it take to destroy a forest?

b) Discuss the destructive effect of an uncontrolled tongue (Jas. 3:6).

QUESTIONS (contd.)

DAY 5 *James 3:7-9.*
a) Put into your own words what verses 7-9 say.

b) How would you describe Cain's answer to God's question in Genesis 4:8-9?

DAY 6 *James 3:9-12.*
a) How are fruit-bearing trees and springs contrasted with the tongue?

b) What do these verses say about the misuse of the tongue: James 1:13-14,26; 2:1-4,15-16; 3:5,14; 4:11-12; 5:12?

DAY 7 How are our tongues to be used? What do the following references suggest: Psalm 150; 51:14; 107:2; Acts 1:8; James 1:5-6; 3:9; 5:13, 17-18?

NOTES

James follows up his statement that true faith is to be evidenced by works by advice to teachers (and us all) that it is also to be evidenced by words. Since a teacher's work is accomplished through words, he warns those who teach others how to live that they will receive more drastic judgment if they have fallen short of their own teaching or cause others to stumble. Scripture also underlines the importance of knowing God's commissioning and the Spirit's enabling in such a task.

A teacher, of necessity, often has to pass moral and intellectual judgments. It is easy for him to slip from *discernment* to *criticism*. No wonder this passage emphasises so clearly that the tongue can be a dangerous weapon. It reveals so clearly the character of the person who uses it. Matthew 12:34 reads: 'For the mouth speaks what the heart is full of' (GNB). So it follows if the heart is evil (untouched and unchanged by the redeeming love of Christ) the tongue cannot speak good. On the other hand, those of us who profess to belong to Christ should speak in such a way that we evidence Christ's control. We are all well aware that this is not always so.

Did you notice in Genesis 4:9 that Cain told God a deliberate lie? All through Scripture we see how easily even those who loved and feared God said wrong, impetuous, even sinful things.

MOSES   'rash words came from Moses' lips' (Ps. 106:33).

ISAIAH   recognised the treachery of his heart and said: 'I am ruined! For I am a man of unclean lips' (Isa. 6:5).

PETER   so emphatic that even if everyone denied Christ, he never would, but later affirmed, 'I don't know the man' (Matt. 26:33-35, 69-75).

There are no answers given to the rhetorical questions in James 3:11-12. The inference, however, is that the Christian should only be using words that edify others and magnify God. But how can he in the light of verse 8, 'but no man can tame the tongue'? In our next study we will find that the Christian's resources are in God.

Romans 6:13 exhorts us to 'offer' ourselves to God and this includes our tongue. Only then can we press on to *maturity* (Jas. 3:2). Here are three things which will keep us if we put them into practice:

A RESOLVE   Psalm 17:3; 39:1.

A WARNING   Matthew 12:34-37.

A PRAYER   Psalm 19:14; 141:3.

STUDY 6
DOES YOUR LIFE RING TRUE?

QUESTIONS

DAY 1 *James 3:13.*
James seems to pick up the theme, begun in 3:1, of teachers.
a) What should be the marks of a wise teacher? Who is he to be like when teaching (Matt. 11:29; 2 Cor. 10:1)?

Brian

b) What similarity is there between verse 13 and James 2:14?

DAY 2 *James 3:14-16.*
a) What two evils does James particularly condemn in a church?

Moma

b) What happens when these two evils are present? What is associated with every disorder in a church?

DAY 3 *James 3:14-16.*
a) What destructive effects of envy are highlighted in the following verses: Matthew 27:18; Acts 5:17-18; 13:45; 1 Corinthians 3:1-4?

Bira

b) Do any of the things that James condemns show up in your life? If you are conscious of 'falling short', what should you do about it (1 John 1:9; Jas. 1:5)?

DAY 4 *James 3:17-18; Galatians 5:22-26.*
a) What is the first characteristic of heavenly wisdom?

Maue

b) What a harvest of good things wisdom produces! List again some of them.

DAY 5 *James 4:1-2.*
a) What was creating conflict for these Christians? What other areas of conflict is a Christian involved in (Rom. 7:23; I Pet. 5:8-9)?

b) What kind of person is described in James 4:2 and why is he like that?

DAY 6 *James 4:3-4.*
a) What has James previously said about unanswered prayer (1:6-7)? What additional reason does he add here?

b) Why is unanswered prayer sometimes a good thing?

c) Between what two friendships are we to choose (Matt. 6:24)? What does James mean when he accuses them of adultery?

DAY 7 *James 4:5-6; Hosea 11:8.*
a) Read James 4:5 in as many translations as possible, then discuss its meaning.

b) What encouragement is there to be humble?

NOTES

Doesn't James drive home the essentials of an effective teacher? He leaves us in no doubt as to the required standards and qualities. He makes clear that spiritual equipping, not academic attainment is to be sought after (Jas. 1:5). The arrogance and unbelief of those who were party to the crucifixion of Christ in John 19 bear out James' point. They acted within the limits of their human wisdom and discernment when they might have seen by the eye of faith, that Jesus was truly the Son of God. The New Bible Commentary, linking James 3:13 and 2:18 says 'wisdom is analogous to faith and must be shown by works'.

'Anyone who says he is a Christian but doesn't control his sharp tongue is just fooling himself, and his religion isn't worth much ... And by all means don't brag about being wise and good if you are bitter and jealous and selfish; that is the worst sort of lie.' This is how the Living Bible presents James 1:26 and 3:14. James majors on the inconsistency of saying we believe but living a lie. Actors in Greek plays were termed 'HYPOCRITES' because in acting, they professed to be something they were not. We can see how the word has been carried into our English language – perhaps better understood today as 'phoney'. This is how Jesus described some of the Pharisees of His day because they said they believed one thing but acted another (Matt. 23). No wonder James condemns this attitude, not only in teachers, but in all believers.

The next few verses reveal clearly the source of such inconsistency. For those who profess to belong to Christ there is only one way to walk and that is in complete devotion and unbroken relationship with Him. Scripture makes it plain that giving in to selfish desire brings areas of conflict into our lives. Paul said, 'What a wretched man I am! Who will rescue me ...' (Rom. 7:24). He knew the tussle of battling against selfish motives and the will of God. Eventually, when God had dealt with him he could say, 'the world has been crucified to me, and I to the world' (Gal. 6:14).

It is quite impossible to produce the fruit of the Spirit (Gal. 5:22-26) while we are lacking in spiritual wisdom and in the humility and purity which this wisdom brings. We have to choose whether we will exalt the Lord or ourselves. Joshua put the challenge to his people: 'choose for yourselves this day whom you will serve ... But as for me and my household, we will serve the Lord' (Josh. 24:15).

2 Corinthians 11:2 brings to us the challenge of Christ through Paul: 'I am jealous for you with a godly jealousy. I promised you to one husband, to Christ, so that I might present you as a pure virgin to him.' Isn't the Lord worthy of your undivided loyalty and devotion?

STUDY 7
CAPITULATE TO CHRIST

QUESTIONS

DAY 1 *James 4:6-7; Matthew 26:38-42; Romans 9:20-21; Hebrews 12:7-11.*
a) Does human nature find it easy to submit? Why?

b) Give reasons from these references why we should submit to God.

DAY 2 *James 4:7; Matthew 4:8-10; John 8:44; 1 Peter 5:8-9.*
a) Why must Christians resist the devil?

b) How are we to do this?

DAY 3 *James 4:8; Deuteronomy 4:7; Hebrews 4:15-16; 10:19-22.*
a) Why is it possible to draw near to God now?

b) Discuss the things that can hinder our close fellowship with God.

DAY 4 *James 4:8; 1:8; 1 John 1:7-8; 3:3.*
a) What does James call these Christians?

b) What did James call on them to do? What difference would there be between the 'washing' of James 4:8 and that in Mark 7:3-4?

QUESTIONS (contd.)

DAY 5 *James 4:9-10.*
a) Discuss the close agreement of verse 9 with Isaiah 6:5-7; Matthew 5:4; 2 Corinthians 7:9-10.

Marie

b) Is a Christian to go around always being mournful (Ps. 51:12)?

DAY 6 *James 4:10.*
a) How does God respond to our humility?

b) What part does the Holy Spirit play in our humility before God (John 16:8)?

Buon

c) How did Jesus illustrate the value of humility in Luke 14:7-11?

DAY 7 *James 4:11-12; Matthew 7:1.*
a) Why is slander against a fellow believer forbidden?

b) What were the people reminded about God? Why do you think James pointed this out?

Joan

c) Matthew 22:37-40; 1 Corinthians 13:4-7. If we slander others, what is missing in our lives?

NOTES

With a few brief sentences James paints a picture of the human heart at variance with God, itself and others. He graphically gets across to us that human pride is the source of all this trouble (Jas. 4:1-6). Quietly he slips in some very important words: 'God ... gives grace to the humble' and goes on to show us the steps to take to remedy the mess that human nature lands us in.

The commentaries describe grace as 'unmerited favour' and a quick look at these references show us that its *source* is God (1 Tim. 6:17); it *saves* (Eph. 2:8-10), *sanctifies* (2 Cor. 8:9), *sustains* (2 Cor. 12:8-9), *equips* for *service* (2 Cor. 9:8).

Did you trace the commands given in James 4:6-12?

SUBMIT (4:7). Get down off the pedestal of pride. We are to be humble as Jesus was humble (Matt. 11:29); as Paul had to be humbled from his self-sufficiency (1 Cor. 15:9; Eph. 3:8; 1 Tim. 1:15). Read 1 Peter 5:5-6 and ask God to make this real in your life.

RESIST (v. 7). Stand up to the devil. He is always on the war path (1 Pet. 5:8-9), full of all kinds of ruses and deception (John 8:44) to tempt us to sin and cause us to stumble. Read Matthew 16:23 and ask God to enable you to resist Satan as Christ did.

COME NEAR (v. 8). Hebrews 4:16 gives the same instruction. God has provided the way in Christ that we might draw near. Have you?

PURIFY (v. 8). Inward cleansing through Christ's atoning work brings a cleansed way of life. Read 2 Corinthians 7:1 and ask the Lord Jesus to make you holy.

REPENT (v. 9). The prerequisite to cleansing is a heart, not only sorry for sin, but abhorring it and determined to forsake it (Acts 3:19). Read Psalm 34:18. Have you walked this way?

CAPITULATE (v. 10). James must be very aware that pride is a great stumbling block in our lives and a hindrance to fellowship, for he keeps introducing this theme. Pride and humility just cannot live together. Read 1 Peter 5:3 and pray for grace to capitulate to Christ.

DO NOT SLANDER (v. 11). If we earnestly pray for each other and walk in humility we will avoid the trap of slandering or judging others. To judge is to deem ourselves better than others and equal with God (v. 12). Humility brings us into a true relationship with God and our fellow men. Read Matthew 7:1-5. How can we attain to these standards? Only by relying on His grace (v. 6).

28st.
Aque

STUDY 8
LIFE – GOD'S WAY

QUESTIONS

DAY 1 *James 4:13-14; Proverbs 27:1.*
a) Do you think it is wrong for a Christian to plan ahead?

b) Luke 12:16-21. What did this rich man forget to plan for?

DAY 2 *James 4:13; Psalm 39:4-6; 90:3-10; 103:14-16.*
a) What are we reminded about in these verses?

b) Should these facts about life depress a Christian (Phil. 1:21)?

DAY 3 *James 4:15; Acts 18:21; 1 Corinthians 4:19; 16:7; Philippians 2:19, 24.*
a) How is Paul's attitude to life an illustration of what James teaches us to do?

b) Why is it important to get into line with God's will for our lives (Prov. 19:21)?

DAY 4 *James 4:16; Proverbs 20:14; Romans 1:30; 1 John 2:16.*
a) What is associated with boasting in these verses?

b) Galatians 6:14. What aspect of boasting is recommended here?

JAMES • STUDY 8 • LIFE – GOD'S WAY • . . . .

QUESTIONS (contd.)

DAY 5 *James 4:17.*
a) How is sin defined here?

b) What other definitions of sin are given in Romans 3:23; I John 3:4?

DAY 6 *James 4:17.*
Think back and try and pick out one 'good' thing we are commanded to do from each chapter so far studied.

DAY 7 *James 4:17; Matthew 25:14-30.*
a) How does the reading from Matthew illustrate the teaching from James?

b) John 13:2-5, 15-17. Why is there an onus on Christians to be faithful in doing even the menial tasks?

NOTES

Puff!
Life can be over, just like that (Jas. 4:14). Does that worry you, or are you living with the expectancy and joy of eternity in fellowship with the Lord Jesus? Compare I Samuel 20:3 with I John 2:25.

Who runs your life?
Paul initially ran his own life (see Acts 26:9-14) but when he eventually came to grips with the Lordship of Christ, he gave over its control to Him (Acts 9:5-6). Read again the portion in Luke 12:16-21 and underline the pronoun 'I'. Scripture clearly shows that the life that swings on the fulcrum of 'I' takes a downward course, but for those who make Christ central, life has a full and eternal meaning. Africans in the Uganda revival some years ago made this the prayer of their hearts:

'Lord bend this proud and stiff-necked I;
Help me to bow the knee and die
Beholding Thee on Calvary, who bowed the neck for me.'

Are you afraid to pray this way, or have you seen that the secret of a happy, fulfilled life is capitulation to His claim of Lordship?

What is the quality of your life?
In the last few verses of chapter 4, James lifts the curtain and reveals something more of the sins and shortcomings of the human heart. It is just so easy for us to live for now and leave eternity out of our reckoning. Materialism (v. 13), self-centred boasting (v. 16), deliberate sinning (v. 17), presumption (vv. 13-17), (note that the Greek word is interpreted as 'shameless and irreverent daring') and last of all, doublemindedness (v. 8) rob us of direction and make decision-making a problem.

Key to stability
The only thing that will deliver us from fear and the uncertainty of life and give us stability in our Christian walk is to learn to yield wholly to God as Paul did. As we are drawn into a consistent attitude of saying 'not as I will, but as you will' many of our problems will dissolve.

'Sweet will of God, still draw me closer ...
Till I am *wholly* lost, in Thee.'

STUDY 9
WISDOM ABOUT WEALTH

QUESTIONS

DAY 1 *James 1:10; 4:13; 5:1.*
a) Do you think James denounces people simply for being rich?

b) What pitfalls do wealthy Christians (and all who aspire to be!) need especially to be on guard against (1 Tim. 6:17-19; Rev. 3:17-18)?

DAY 2 *James 5:1-6.*
a) What evils were these rich landowners guilty of?

b) What evils do you think James would condemn in our society today?

DAY 3 *James 5:1-6,9.*
a) Why should these rich people have been very concerned after hearing what James had to say (Ps. 10:13-14)?

b) Job 1:20-23; Acts 20:32-35. How can these verses help shape our attitude to material things?

DAY 4 *James 5:7; Deuteronomy 11:13-17.*
a) How reliant is the farmer on things beyond his control?

b) What quality does this produce in him?

QUESTIONS (contd.)

DAY 5 *James 5:7-9; Matthew 7:1-2; 2 Peter 3:10-12a.*
a) What imminent event does James mention here?

b) What three things are Christians told to do in the light of this?

DAY 6 *James 5:10-11; Acts 7:52.*
a) Can you remember what encouragement James has already given in chapter 1 about persevering under trials (vv. 4, 12)?

b) What does James add now to this?

DAY 7 *James 5:12; Matthew 5:34-37.*
a) Discuss the probable link between James' injunction to be patient (v. 8) and not to swear (v. 12).

b) How would you express the last part of verse 12?

NOTES

In the last part of chapter 4 James denounces the self-confident habit of planning one's own life. Now he proceeds to emphasise the futility of putting confidence in riches. The stress here is not that wealth is wrong, rather James is talking about wealth wrongfully acquired and misused.

Read the story of Lazarus and the rich man (Luke 16:19-31) which clearly reveals the end of one who has lived a self-indulgent, heartless life. Also read the parable of the prodigal son (Luke 15:11-20) and how he learned, through bitter experience, the right perspective on riches.

Job, James and Paul had the right attitude to materialism and the warning given to the Laodicean Church in Revelation 3 is surely a message for those of us who don't have the right outlook on riches today.

Having stressed the right attitude of the Christian to wealth in the light of the coming judgment, James reverts to his original message of faith under trial and exhorts us to be patient because the Lord Jesus will soon come again. He illustrates his message by referring to the farmer who is utterly dependent on the God of the elements for the production of his crops. In Palestine there are two seasons of rain interspersed with a period of dry weather. The first rain softens the ground for sowing, the second waters the thirsty crop. The farmer can do nothing but wait patiently through this process. So we too are to be patient till Jesus comes, encouraging each other, strengthening our hearts (see also Heb. 10:24-25) and not grumbling. Exodus 15:24 and subsequent chapters tell how the Israelites sinned by constantly complaining despite God's goodness. In John 6:43 Jesus Himself tells us not to grumble or complain.

DISCOURAGED?

Go to the Bible. Read of others who were tempted to grumble and despair and see how they overcame. Read Hebrews 11 and be encouraged to prove God faithful in your circumstances too. Most of all, remember, Jesus has walked the same human pathway, fully understands and stands by to strengthen us (see I Pet. 2:21 and Heb. 2:18).

26th May.

STUDY 10
APPLYING SPIRITUAL PRINCIPLES

QUESTIONS

DAY 1 _James 5:13-20._
From these verses list the activities and attitudes you would expect to find in a Christian Church.

Bira

DAY 2 _James 5:13-16._
a) What is the main emphasis of these verses?

audrey

b) Can you find three types of prayer in this passage?

DAY 3 _Psalm 66:18; Matthew 5:23-24; Mark 11:25-26; James 4:3; 1 Peter 3:7._
a) What, in these references, makes prayer ineffective?

Christine

b) Perhaps you would like to have a few moments of silent prayer (share together if you want) and ask the Holy Spirit to reveal any prayer hindrance in your life.

DAY 4 _James 5:16-18._
a) Whose prayers are very 'powerful and effective' (compare translations)?

Maria

b) What is very encouraging from this reference to Elijah?

33

QUESTIONS (contd.)

DAY 5 *Read the following references and write in what resulted from prayer in each instance:*
a) I Kings 17:1 (Jas. 4:17) and Acts 4:29-31.

Mykio . ~~Prayer directed at god~~ Boldness to speak out

b) I Kings 17:2-6 and Philippians 4:19.

food & water given

c) I Kings 17:17-24 and Mark 11:22-24.

god's power re healed

DAY 6 *James 5:13; Acts 16:25.*
a) What do these references teach us about praise?

Norma
b) James 5:16; Philippians 1:19. What aspect of intercession is highlighted here?

DAY 7 *James 5:19-20.*
James closes with two practical considerations.
a) What should we be careful to avoid?

Brian)

b) What should we be conscientious in doing?

c) How can meeting together regularly to study the Bible achieve both aims?

NOTES

Prayer

These few verses certainly impress us with the importance of prayer in *every circumstance* of life. This week's study gives just a glimpse into this all-important area of the Christian's life. From the few references given in the study we begin to realise that God does hear and answer prayer and has made provision for our every human need.

Relationships

Prayer, to be effective, must rise from a *believing heart* (Matt. 21:22) right with God (I Pet. 3:12) and *right with others* (Matt. 5:23-24). One of the most helpful passages to study on this is I John 1:7, 9 which graphically bears out the need for the Christian to know *continual cleansing* through *continual confession* and *appropriation of Christ's cleansing.* This is the only way to unbroken fellowship with God and fellow Christians.

Facets of Prayer

I Thessalonians 5:16-17 emphasises what James says in 5:13 and shows the importance of continual *praise* as well as *prayer.* Only the heart at peace with God and accepting His will is at liberty to praise. Paul and Silas praised while in prison (Acts 16:25). When hearts are right, feelings and circumstances can't stop us praising. Praise will help us out of despair and depression so long as we've applied the principles of forgiveness and fellowship.

Prayer can take many forms – a heavenly telegram in a moment of emergency – simple laying of our needs before God – desperate pleading with God to reveal His way through a problem – intense intercession for another in a tough spot (maybe a missionary?) – bearing up a loved one undergoing sickness or trial – pleading for enlightenment for those in spiritual darkness. If you set yourself to a Scriptural study of prayer God will teach you. Remember too, that Jesus is constantly praying for us (Heb. 7:25).

Concern and Compassion

It is fitting at the close of this book after all James' instruction on being *practical* in our *faith,* that he encourages us to be active soul winners. Included in these final verses is the injunction to yearn over and seek for the restoration of backsliders – as our Lord yearned over Israel (Hos. 4:1-4).

Was James thinking of Proverbs 11:30 as he finished his epistle? His opening exhortation was to seek heavenly wisdom. Have we taken by faith this wisdom? Are we walking in the experience (faith that works) that 'he who wins souls is wise'?

ANSWER GUIDE

The following pages contain an Answer Guide. It is recommended that answers to the questions be attempted before turning to this guide. It is only a guide and the answers given should not be treated as exhaustive.

GUIDE TO STUDY 1

DAY 1   a) Perfect or mature.
b) Inability to cope with even the simple basics of God's work; carnality, quarrelling, arguing, envy, etc.

DAY 2   a) Faith, becoming part of God's family (a 'brother').
b) We need to receive, or believe in the Lord Jesus. It does not come about through any natural process or privilege.

DAY 3   a) He refers to them as brothers.
b) Belonging to God's family brings privileges of love and fellowship and obligates us to be patient, loving, encouraging and forbearing with each other. (See Rom. 12:4-5; Eph. 4:2; Matt. 18:21; Col. 3:13; etc.)

DAY 4   a) A servant of God and the Lord Jesus Christ.
b) Salvation delivers us from sin, and the continuing work of God's Spirit delivers us from being self-centred, making us God-centred people. Since God both made us and then bought us back through Christ, we are really His twice over.

DAY 5   a) To submit to and be humble before God.
b) We become more aware and concerned for them.

DAY 6   a) Trials and discipline lead to spiritual growth and maturity.
b) No one welcomes testing, but we should try to see the moulding hand of God and rejoice that He is dealing with us as sons.

DAY 7   a) Christians will be rewarded in heaven; they will receive 'the crown of life'.
b) That they continue to love Him.

JAMES • ANSWER GUIDE • • • • • • •

GUIDE TO STUDY 2

DAY 1 a) Human (earthly) and heavenly wisdom.
b) Human or earthly wisdom produces jealousy, rivalry, sensuality, confusion and everything base.
Heavenly or spiritual wisdom results in purity, peace, courtesy, mercy, congeniality, impartiality, sincerity, producing only good fruits.
Surely we desire the latter.

DAY 2 a) God will give it willingly and generously.
b) God would meet every need of the believers.

DAY 3 a) Lack of faith, doubting God and His Word.
b) To be totally committed to God (thus leaving no room for doubt) and to approach God with faith.

DAY 4 a) The poor and the rich Christian.
The poor are to rejoice probably because of their riches in Christ. The rich are to rejoice or take pride in their 'low' position. As Christians they probably were now being persecuted. They were better in this position rather than being popular without God.
b) Death can come quickly and unexpectedly to the rich. Riches alone do not prepare them for the future.

DAY 5 a) The tempter – the devil.
b) When we give in to covetous or lustful desires.

DAY 6 a) To avoid taking any responsibility for what they had done. James is quite emphatic that God will not tempt anyone to do evil. He is holy.
b) God has provided us with a Saviour who overcame all temptation and fortifies us to stand against the tempter. We are to humbly yield to God and resist the devil. We are to look for God's way out.

DAY 7 a) God is unchangeable and our Creator; He is a Father who gives the very best to His children; He acts according to His divine will.
b) By reading and listening to what the Bible says; by putting what James has to say into practice.

GUIDE TO STUDY 3

DAY 1 a) It is something that originates with God. It is not something we grow into but something that God does for us when we believe.
b) Either the promise of more fruit to follow (Christ's death and resurrection has resulted in a rich harvest of souls for God) or something specially favoured by God.

DAY 2 a) Personal.
b) It is not conducive to a holy life; it is closely linked with other sinful habits.

DAY 3 a) The need to separate from what is sinful, and the need for time and obedience to be given to God's Word.
b) It brings us salvation and makes us productive disciples.

DAY 4 a) We are deceiving ourselves.
b) He used the illustration of the wise and foolish builders and the consequences of their actions for each one.

DAY 5 a) A mirror.
b) As one who glances without acting and later forgets.

DAY 6 a) They are blessed in all they do.
They constantly apply themselves to finding out what is in God's Word and they are careful not to forget what it says.
b) Fruitfulness and favour with God.

DAY 7 a) What we say reveals what we are.
b) Practical concern for the needy and personal holiness.

GUIDE TO STUDY 4

DAY 1   a) The sin of showing favouritism.
People were being allocated seats based on their outward appearances.
b) Many types: racial, age, sex, etc.

DAY 2   a) We should see the poor who are believers as God sees them, 'rich in faith'. The rich deserve no favours as they show no mercy to anyone.
b) That of being slandered or blasphemed against because of being a Christian.

DAY 3   a) This 'royal law' of always loving our neighbour as ourselves.
b) God requires perfect, not partial, obedience. Failure to love still means we have broken the law even though not as murderers.

DAY 4   a) Their faith implies that they will show practical concern for others.
b) By coming (like the tax collector in Luke 18) to God in repentance, humility and faith.
No; we are saved through God's mercy and grace alone.

DAY 5   a) Our actions. Putting what we SAY we believe into PRACTICE.
b) He believed God and so obeyed Him even to the point of sacrificing the 'son of promise'.

DAY 6   a) She knew that her city was doomed and that any hope of survival lay with the God of Israel. She believed Israel's God was the true God to the extent that she ACTED on what she BELIEVED.
b) She and her household were saved.

DAY 7   a) Discuss the specific actions of Zacchaeus, Lydia and the Jailer, but stress that they acted on what they BELIEVED.
b) Discuss James 2 and the emphasis put upon GOOD WORKS resulting from a LIVING FAITH in Christ.

GUIDE TO STUDY 5

DAY 1   a) They are accountable to God and are to be judged severely if their teaching causes others to stumble.
b) That he has been called and equipped by God for the task.

DAY 2   a) They reveal our thoughts, an indication of what we really are.
b) He can control his whole body, that is, he is perfect or mature.

DAY 3   a) They are all small and yet have power to direct.
b) By a master hand on the very small rudder.

DAY 4   a) Big fires start with a small spark.
b) The sinfulness of unregenerate nature finds expression through the tongue, polluting the personality and continuously and adversely influencing the whole course of life; such action sparks off in hell and leads to final condemnation (Matt. 5:22).

DAY 5   a) Man can bring living creatures under control, but is powerless to control his own tongue. One moment he can be blessing God – the next – cursing men!
b) An outright lie!

DAY 6   a) A fruit tree produces one kind of fruit and a spring one kind of water, but the tongue is capable of producing both blessing and cursing.
b) It can be used to blame God and speak hypocritically; speak unfeelingly to people in need; boast and flatter so as to cause trouble; speak evil of others; swear and blaspheme.

DAY 7   To praise God in word and song.
Pray for our own needs and the needs of others to be supplied.
To witness for the Lord.

GUIDE TO STUDY 6

DAY 1   a) An exemplary lifestyle, deeds flowing from humility. The Lord Jesus.
b) Both faith and wisdom are to be characterised by deeds and not simply words.

DAY 2   a) Envy and selfish ambition.
b) Disorder and sinful practices exist.
Demonic activity.

DAY 3   a) Religious leaders wanted to get rid of Jesus; persecutions; hindrances to the Gospel; divisions and no spiritual growth in a church.
b) Personal. Ask God for cleansing and wisdom.

DAY 4   a) It is pure (and the life controlled by it is likewise changed).
b) Peace, gentleness, reasonableness, mercy, good fruit (Gal. 5:22), impartiality and sincerity (not hypocritical).

DAY 5   a) Selfish desires. The battle of the mind and that against the devil.
b) A thoroughly discontented and unsatisfied person. He hasn't complied with James 1:5.

DAY 6   a) It is due to a lack of faith.
It is due to asking with wrong or selfish motives.
b) We might have asked for some selfish thing which, if we had received it, would have hindered us spiritually.
c) Between siding with God or the world.
He is referring to Christians who allow selfish desires to disrupt their relationship with Christ. The conflicting friendships of James 4:4 are incompatible.

DAY 7   a) God yearns over us with godly jealousy; He longs for our undivided devotion.
b) God resists the proud but gives 'grace' to the humble.

GUIDE TO STUDY 7

DAY 1 a) No. By nature we all tend to be proud and independent.
b) God commands it; Jesus exemplified it; God is our Creator; for the Christian, God is his Father and acts for his good.

DAY 2 a) He is diametrically opposed to the worship of God and truth; his intentions are destructive: he seeks to maim Christians in their walk and witness and rob them of joy.
b) Be submissive to God; be aware of his activity; use the Word of God and pray.

DAY 3 a) The sacrifice (the shed blood) of the Lord Jesus has removed the obstacle of our sin that was separating us from God.

b) Any sin, pride, lack of faith, neglect of prayer and the Word of God, etc.

DAY 4 a) Sinners, double-minded (answers will depend on translation used).
b) To seek cleansing.
The Pharisees were only interested in external, ceremonial cleansing. James may be thinking of this picture but is obviously referring to a deeper cleansing that can only come through the blood of Jesus.

DAY 5 a) A consciousness of, and sorrow for, sin always precedes cleansing and blessing.
b) No; David expected his joy in the Lord to be restored.

DAY 6 a) He sees it, draws near to us and will 'lift' us up.
b) He will point out our sin, lack of humility, etc., if we allow Him.
c) The humble person becomes the honoured person.

DAY 7 a) It is breaking God's law (Exod. 20:16) thus showing contempt for it; it assumes a position of superiority over the person slandered, a position which is not possible as only God can exercise this function.
b) James puts emphasis on who God is (Judge, Omnipotent). Our conduct is closely related to what we believe about God.
c) Love for God and others.

GUIDE TO STUDY 8

DAY 1   a) Not if it is done prayerfully and with an attitude of heart that bows to God's overruling wisdom and direction.
b) God, his eternal destiny, the brevity of life.

DAY 2   a) The brevity and uncertainty of life.
b) No; he has prospects of eternal life in heaven.

DAY 3   a) Paul readily acknowledged the supremacy of God in the affairs of men and desired God's way for himself.
b) Anything less than God's will leads to failure and frustration.

DAY 4   a) Evil and conduct reprehensible to God.
b) Our rejoicing should be in Christ and His victory through the cross. In this way we exalt Jesus and not ourselves.

DAY 5   a) Not doing what we know we should be doing.
b) Not being up to God's standard of holiness; lawlessness.

DAY 6   Suggestions: be obedient to God's Word (Jas. 1:22); respect the poor (Jas. 2:1); promote peace (Jas. 3:17-18); pray with right motives (Jas. 4:3).

DAY 7   a) The servants were expected to use their talents. The servant who did nothing was labelled 'wicked and lazy' and was judged.
b) Jesus has set an example for us. Blessings are promised to those who do them.

GUIDE TO STUDY 9

DAY 1   a) Not necessarily. He is using these verses to warn against the fleeting nature of riches and possible abuse of them.
b) False sense of security; love of power; being more taken up with what this life can give than with the Kingdom of God; ruthlessness (overriding others in the desire to get more).

DAY 2   a) Self-indulgence; taking advantage of the poor to accumulate for themselves. They were ruthless and prepared to murder.
b) Personal.

DAY 3   a) God was taking note of their evil conduct; there is a day of reckoning implied.
b) We should realise that material things are God-given and that He can withdraw them. We need to avoid being covetous and instead be diligent in helping others.

DAY 4   a) Utterly dependent on the God who controls the elements for the production of their crops.
b) Patience.

DAY 5   a) The coming of the Lord.
b) Wait patiently (as the farmer waits for the maturing crop), stand firm and not grumble against each other.

DAY 6   a) Personal.
b) Many (even prophets) have suffered in the past and we can learn from their example. This can be done through reading Scripture or Christian biographies. God is 'full of compassion and mercy'. Job is an example of one who suffered and then was blessed.

DAY 7   a) Impatience, anger and lack of self-control predispose us to unwise use of our tongues, even to 'taking the Lord's name in vain'. A Christian should be under the control of Christ and therefore have a 'clean tongue'.
b) 'Say what you mean and mean what you say.'

JAMES • ANSWER GUIDE • • • • • •

GUIDE TO STUDY 10

DAY 1 Prayer under all circumstances; praise; prayerful fellowship with those spiritually and physically sick; sharing; a burden to point others to Christ.

DAY 2 a) An encouragement to pray in every life situation we face.
b) Seeking God for the meeting of my personal need; interceding for others; praise.

DAY 3 a) Unconfessed sin; unwillingness for reconciliation; an unforgiving spirit; selfishness; inconsideration in a marriage relationship.
b) Personal.

DAY 4 a) The prayers of a righteous person.
b) Effective prayer is not restricted to superpeople. Elijah experienced ups and downs in life, yet he persevered in prayer. Elijah prayed and God answered.

DAY 5 a) Boldness was given to speak God's Word.
b) Provision was made for human needs.
c) God's wonder-working power was revealed.

DAY 6 a) Praise needs to be expressed to God and should not be restricted by external circumstances.
b) Praying for particular situations and people.

DAY 7 a) Wandering from the truth.
b) Seeking to restore backsliders.
c) By studying the Bible we are made aware of the truth; sharing with others brings mutual encouragement.

THE WORD WORLDWIDE

We first heard of WORD WORLDWIDE over twenty years ago when Marie Dinnen, its founder, shared excitedly about the wonderful way ministry to one needy woman had exploded to touch many lives. It was great to see the Word of God being made central in the lives of thousands of men and women, then to witness the life-changing results of them applying the Word to their circumstances. Over the years the vision for WORD WORLDWIDE has not dimmed in the hearts of those who are involved in this ministry. God is still at work through His Word and in today's self-seeking society, the Word is even more relevant to those who desire true meaning and purpose in life. WORD WORLDWIDE is a ministry of WEC International, an interdenominational missionary society, whose sole purpose is to see Christ known, loved and worshipped by all, particularly those who have yet to hear of His wonderful name. This ministry is a vital part of our work and we warmly recommend the WORD WORLDWIDE 'Geared for Growth' Bible studies to you. We know that as you study His Word you will be enriched in your personal walk with Christ. It is our hope that as you are blessed through these studies, you will find opportunities to help others discover a personal relationship with Jesus. As a mission we would encourage you to work with us to make Christ known to the ends of the earth.

Stewart and Jean Moulds – British Directors, **WEC International**.

A full list of over 50 'Geared for Growth' studies can be obtained from:

John and Ann Edwards
5 Louvaine Terrace, Hetton-le-Hole, Tyne & Wear, DH5 9PP
Tel. 0191 5262803 Email: rhysjohn.edwards@virgin.net

Anne Jenkins
2 Windermere Road, Carnforth, Lancs., LA5 9AR
Tel. 01524 734797 Email: anne@gearedforgrowth.co.uk

UK Website: www.gearedforgrowth.co.uk

JAMES

Christian Focus Publications

publishes books for all ages

Our mission statement –

STAYING FAITHFUL

In dependence upon God we seek to help make His infallible word, the Bible, relevant. Our aim is to ensure that the Lord Jesus Christ is presented as the only hope to obtain forgiveness of sin, live a useful life and look forward to heaven with Him.

REACHING OUT

Christ's last command requires us to reach out to our world with His gospel. We seek to help fulfil that by publishing books that point people towards Jesus and help them develop a Christ-like maturity. We aim to equip all levels of readers for life, work, ministry and mission.

Books in our adult range are published in three imprints.

Christian Focus contains popular works including biographies, commentaries, basic doctrine, and Christian living. Our children's books are also published in this imprint.

Mentor focuses on books written at a level suitable for Bible College and seminary students, pastors, and other serious readers; the imprint includes commentaries, doctrinal studies, examination of current issues, and church history.

Christian Heritage contains classic writings from the past.

For details of our titles visit us on our website
www.christianfocus.com

ISBN 0-90806-701-1
ISBN 978-0-90806-701-5

Published in 2002
and reprinted in 2007
by
Christian Focus Publications, Geanies House,
Fearn, Ross-shire, IV20 ITW, Scotland
and
WEC International, Bulstrode, Oxford Road,
Gerrards Cross, Bucks, SL9 8SZ

Cover design by Alister MacInnes

Printed and bound by Bell and Bain